Rugby League

Written in association
with the RFL

Produced for A&C Black by

Monkey Puzzle Media Ltd
Gissings Farm, Fressingfield
Suffolk IP21 5SH

Published in 2007 by

A & C Black Publishers Ltd
38 Soho Square, London W1D 3HB
www.acblack.com

Third edition 2007

Copyright © 2007, 2004, 1994 The RFL

ISBN: 978 0 7136 8376 9

A CIP record for this book is available from the British Library.

Note: While every effort has been made to ensure that the content of this book is as technically accurate and as sound as possible, neither the author nor the publisher can accept responsibility for any injury or loss sustained as a result of the use of this material.

This book is produced using paper that is made from wood grown in managed, sustainable forests. It is natural, renewable and recyclable. The logging and manufacturing processes conform to the environmental regulations of the country of origin.

Acknowledgements
Cover and inside design by James Winrow and Tom Morris for Monkey Puzzle Media Ltd.
Cover photograph courtesy of Clint Hughes/PA Archive/PA Photos.
The publishers would like to thank the Andrew Varley Picture Agency of Leeds for their photographic contribution to this book as well as image contributions from the RFL's Marketing and Services Departments (pages 4, 10, 11, 12, 13, 58, 59, 60 and 61). The photograph on page 35 is courtesy of PA Photos.
All illustrations by Dave Saunders.
The publishers would like to extend special thanks to John Huxley for his contribution to this book.

KNOW THE GAME is a registered trademark.

Printed and bound in China by C&C Offset Printing Co., Ltd.

Note: Throughout the book players and officials are referred to as 'he'. This should, of course, be taken to mean 'he or she' where appropriate. Similarly, all instructions are geared towards right-handed players – left-handers should simply reverse these instructions.

CONTENTS

INTRODUCTION

Rugby league is an all-action game that thrills spectators and demands much of players. It features moments of shuddering heavy physical contact contrasted with occasions of incredible pace and delicate skill and flair.

GAME TIME

In an 80-minute game, the ball will be in play for 50 minutes or more, longer than rugby union, and each player will cover between 5 and 7 km (3–4.3 miles) running backwards, jogging and running flat-out. Although teams may have specialist kickers or pacy backs, all players must be able to run at speed, handle and tackle well.

HISTORY

One of the biggest sporting rows of all time led to the formation of rugby league football. Throughout the early 1890s, many rugby union clubs in the north of England were accused of paying players to play or to move to their club. At the time, the game was strictly amateur. Such allegations were seldom proven, but an increasing number of northern clubs wished to make 'broken time' payments to compensate their players for loss of wages.

Australia have won every Rugby League World Cup since 1975.

Rugby league is popular with young players. For them to progress, they must work hard in training, take advice on board, and learn to link their individual flair and skill to excellent teamwork.

In August 1895, 21 clubs voted to break away from the Rugby Football Union and form a new separate body called the 'Northern Rugby Football Union'. At first, they played under rugby union rules. But the need to make the game more exciting and attract spectators and finance saw rule changes. In 1922, the Northern Union changed its name to the Rugby Football League (RFL). Today, rugby league is firmly established as one of the world's major spectator and participant sports.

Top rugby league players need excellent skills, strength, suppleness, stamina (the ability to work hard for long periods) and speed.

PLAYING PROFILE

Whilst the professional game remains strongest in the north of England, professional clubs do exist in the south. At amateur level, rugby league is played throughout England, Scotland, Wales and Northern Ireland and is popular at schools, colleges, universities and in the armed services. During the last decade, women's and girls' rugby league has become increasingly popular and prominent. The Great Britain women's team has competed against Australia and New Zealand.

The UK professional season lasts from March to October.

THE RUGBY LEAGUE WORLD CUP

The Rugby League World Cup was first held in France in 1954. Four nations, France, Australia, New Zealand and Great Britain, competed. Changes to the competition occurred over the years and in 2000, 16 teams including Russia, Lebanon, Tonga and Fiji took part. The 2008 competition in Australia will feature ten teams.

THE GAME

The game of rugby league is played by two teams, each with 13 players. The object of the game is to score tries and kick goals. The team with the most points wins.

SCORING

A try is scored by a player grounding the ball in his opponents' in-goal area (see diagram below). A goal is scored by kicking the ball between the opponents' goalposts and above the crossbar. The points scored are as follows:

- a try – four points

- a conversion or a penalty goal – two points

- a field goal – one point.

THE FIELD

The playing area should be as near as possible to the maximum dimensions, although smaller pitches are allowed for youngsters' games. Minimum dimensions are given in the rules governing a particular league or competition. Marking lines should be clear and uniform in width and not more than 100mm wide.

 This diagram illustrates the markings and dimensions of the playing area.

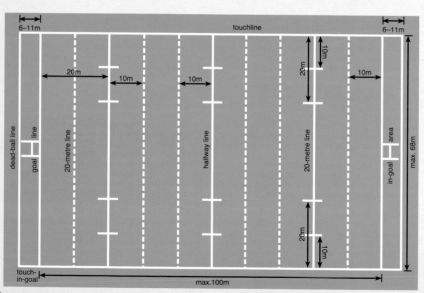

GOALPOSTS

On each goal line and an equal distance from each touchline are two upright posts joined by a crossbar, called goalposts. Dimensions are shown in the diagram at the bottom of this page. The crossbar must not extend beyond the goalposts. Clubs must wrap foam pads around the bases of the posts as protection for the players.

FLAGPOSTS

Posts with a flag are placed at the corners of the goal line and the touchline. They must be made of non-rigid material and be at least 1.2m high.

PLAYERS AND SUBSTITUTES

There are 13 players on either teams at the start of play. Four extra players per side are nominated as substitutes and, in the professional game, team head coaches are allowed to use these players to make as many as 12 interchanges during the match. These interchanges also include 'blood-bin' changes where players who are bleeding have to leave the field for treatment. This is now the internationally accepted method of substitutions during the 80 minutes played during the game.

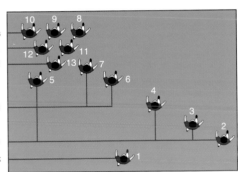

front row forwards
second row forwards
loose forward

Players' positions.

half-backs

three-quarter backs

full back

The goalposts are considered to extend indefinitely upwards. A kick that sails above the goalposts but in line between them is still a goal.

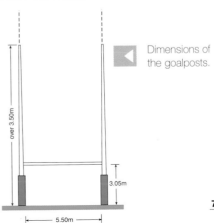

Dimensions of the goalposts.

over 3.50m

3.05m

5.50m

EQUIPMENT

A player's equipment consists of jersey, shorts, socks and studded boots. The players of one side all wear the same coloured jerseys and shorts. These are usually numbered with the number indicating the position of the wearer. Many players choose to wear specially designed support or protective clothing such as shoulder pads. This can protect against injury during a game or to prevent a previous injury being damaged further whilst playing. Head protectors, sometimes known as 'scrum caps', are worn by some players. All such protective equipment should be of a design approved by the governing body's medical panel.

It is the duty of the referee to order a player to remove any part of his equipment which is likely to cause injury to other players. This could involve rings on fingers, other jewellery or projecting nails on boots.

Gum shield

It is strongly recommended that a gum shield is worn to act as a shock absorber for the mouth. The gum shield should be individually tailored to a player's dental profile by an orthodontist.

Boots and studs

On relatively firm ground, shorter boot studs are used. Long studs are more useful on soft ground. Studs on boots must be a minimum of 8mm in diameter at their apex (the end of the stud that first touches the ground). If they are made of metal, they must have rounded edges.

The ball

The oval ball used in rugby league has an air-inflated bladder covered in an outer casing made of leather or another approved material. If the ball becomes deflated during play, the referee should blow the whistle to stop the game until that ball is re-inflated or a new ball provided.

A rugby league player may cover many kilometres during a game. It makes sense, then, to take care of your boots, cleaning and softening them with polish after every game.

The ability to break tackles is a valuable skill in rugby league. Getting past the 'gain line' – the imaginary line across the pitch where the move started – is what wins matches.

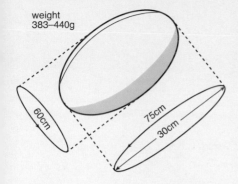

weight
383–440g

60cm

75cm

30cm

A rugby league ball is oval and has a maximum length of approximately 30cm and weighs between 383 and 440g. Maximum circumference at its widest point – 60cm. Maximum circumference at its longest point – 75cm.

COLOUR CLASH

The referee's clothing should be of a colour easily distinguishable and not clashing with the players' jerseys. The referee can act if he thinks that the similarity between the colours of the jersey of the two sides is likely to cause confusion. He may instruct the away side to use jerseys of a different colour.

THE OFFICIALS

All matches are controlled by an appointed referee and two touch judges, who are under the control of the referee.

THE REFEREE

The referee is responsible for the control of the game. He enforces the laws during play, is the sole timekeeper, unless timekeepers are appointed, and keeps a record of the scores.

The referee should carry:

- a whistle that is blown to stop play
- a spare whistle
- a notebook
- pencils
- a coin
- a stopwatch.

▼ Referees use a variety of signals to communicate their decisions to players and match officials (see pages 37 and 38). Here, the referee has awarded a penalty kick.

THE REFEREE'S ROLE

The success of the game depends largely on the referee, who should keep up with the play, be neutral at all times in his decisions, and limit stoppages to a minimum. The players are under the control of the referee from the time they enter the playing area until the time they leave it.

The referee may:

- allow extra time for delays and time wasted
- suspend a game if he thinks it necessary
- dismiss from the field of play any player who persistently and deliberately breaks the laws

Learn all the referee's signals so that you can be aware of his decisions during a game.

- dismiss from the field of play any player who is guilty of foul play or misconduct.

Having given a decision the referee cannot alter it unless a new decision on an earlier incident is required such as when a touch judge reports to the referee that the ball has been in touch.

Sin bin

If, in the referee's judgement, a player is guilty of misconduct of a less serious nature, he may impose a temporary dismissal under which the guilty player must leave the field of play for 10 minutes (the 'sin bin').

Blood bin

If a player is bleeding profusely the referee must order him to leave the field for treatment. During his absence a substitute may take his place, but that substitution is counted towards one of the team's 12 allowable interchanges during the game.

On report

Reports of all untoward incidents are forwarded by the referee to the organisation under the jurisdiction of which the game is being played. In professional games, if a referee is unsure what happened during an incident he can mark the incident by placing the player or players 'on report'. This means the incident will be judged by the authorities at a later date.

THE FOURTH OFFICIAL

In all professional games a fourth official, called the reserve referee, is on hand. He can administer sin-bin and blood-bin situations. He can also take over from the original referee if he becomes injured or cannot continue running the game.

 Touch judges signal a kick at goal by raising their flags.

THE VIDEO REFEREE

In televised matches, the officials are assisted by a video referee. If the match referee is uncertain whether a try has been scored he refers the incident to the video referee who watches slow motion replays. He advises the match referee whether a score has been made.

TOUCH JUDGES

The touch judge decides where the ball goes out of play and into touch. He also judges kicks at goal and may call the referee's attention to any foul play which escaped the referee's notice.

Finding touch

To indicate that a player has 'found touch' a touch judge runs to the point where the ball enters touch. He stands there with flag upraised until the game restarts. The game is restarted by a scrum formed on the 20-metre line opposite where the touch judge stands except in the case of a penalty kick to touch (see page 16).

If the ball is kicked forwards and enters touch 'on the full' (without bouncing on the pitch), the touch judge indicates 'ball back' by waving his flag backwards and forwards above his head. In this case the game is restarted by forming a scrum where the ball was kicked (see page 16).

Team captains determine the choice of ends with a coin toss. The home captain tosses a coin in the presence of the referee, giving the visiting captain the call.

DURATION OF THE GAME

In senior competitions, a rugby league game lasts 80 minutes. It is divided into two equal halves with a 10 minute half-time interval. At half-time the teams change ends. The referee blows his whistle to indicate half-time or full-time. He should not blow for half-time or full-time until the ball is out of play or a player in possession has been tackled.

Allowing time

If a penalty kick has been awarded, the referee must allow it to be taken before blowing for half-time or full-time. Time should be extended to allow for a second kick to be taken if the penalty kick was kicked into touch.

Choice of ends

The winner of a coin toss before the game can choose which goal his team will defend, or to take the kick-off. After the interval the kick-off is taken by the team which did not kick off the first half.

The touch judge flag signals when the ball has found touch and ball back situations.

POSITION AT PENALTY KICKS

When a penalty kick is taken, the nearer touch judge takes up a position near the touchline 10m beyond the mark to show where the defending team have to retire. He waves his flag horizontally in front of him if any player fails to retire the required 10m.

When a kick at goal is successful, the touch judge raises his flag above his head. He signals 'no goal' by waving his flag across the front of his body below his waist.

13

KICK-OFF AND BALL-IN-PLAY RULES

All games of rugby league are started with a kick-off. Whenever the players are taking part in the progress of the game, it is called keeping the ball in play.

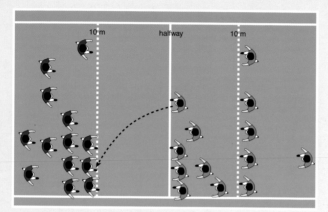

The team receiving the kick-off (red shirts) must retreat behind their 10m mark until the ball is kicked forward.

THE KICK-OFF

After the choice of ends, the teams line up in their respective halves of the field. The game is started by a place kick taken by the side awarded the kick-off. The ball is placed at the centre of the halfway line and must be kicked forwards beyond the opponents' 10m mark. All players on the kicker's side must remain behind the halfway line until after the ball has been kicked forwards. The game is restarted in a similar way:

- after points have been scored
- at the start of the second half of the game.

When the ball is kicked off, the kicker must kick the ball 10m forwards and no one on his side may touch the ball before it has travelled 10m forwards. Any infringement of this rule will result in a penalty kick being awarded against the kicker's side at the centre of the halfway line.

After kick-off

After kick-off, the ball may be kicked or picked up by any player. A player may 'find touch' from the kick-off, provided that the ball travels at least 10m forwards and bounces in the field of play before crossing the touchline. If he kicks directly over the touchline, however, a penalty is awarded against him. This also applies should the ball be kicked dead on the full. In both cases a penalty kick at the centre of the halfway line is awarded against the offending team.

BALL IN AND OUT OF PLAY

The ball is out of play when it goes into touch, is made 'dead', or when the referee stops the game.

Touch
The ball is in touch when:

- it touches the ground on or over the touchline

- even though the ball itself is still in play, it is touched by a player who is himself in touch

- a player carrying it steps on or touches the touchline or the ground outside the touchline.

The ball is not in touch and remains in play when:

- it crosses the touchline in the air but swerves or is blown back into the field of play before bouncing

- a player standing inside the field of play reaches over the touchline and catches the ball before it touches the ground.

When the ball goes into touch in regular play or is carried over the touchline by a player, a scrum is formed opposite the point where the ball crossed or touched the line and 20m inside the field of play.

The ball is spilled and heads out of play, about to cross the side touchline.

Finding touch

A player can gain ground by finding touch – kicking the ball forwards so that it first bounces in the field of play before entering touch. In this case a scrum is formed opposite the point where the ball crossed the touchline, 20m inside the field. At the scrum, the non-kicking side has the advantage of the loose head (see page 28) and feed the ball into the scrum unless it is a 40-20 (see below).

40-20

A 40-20 occurs when a player kicks the ball from behind their own 40-metre line and it enters touch within the opposition's 20-metre area. If this occurs, the kicking team have the advantage of the loose head and feed the ball into the scrum.

Ball back

Apart from at a penalty kick, a player cannot gain ground by kicking the ball forwards into touch without the ball bouncing. This is known as ball back and a scrum is formed where the ball was kicked. One exception is when a ball back situation occurs from a place kick from the centre of the pitch. In this situation, a penalty is awarded against the kicker.

Kicking the ball

If a player kicks the ball from his own in-goal and it goes into touch on the full, the game is restarted with a drop-out from between the posts.

A player is allowed to find touch with a kick from his own in-goal providing the ball bounces in the field of play before going into touch.

Dead ball

The game is restarted with a drop kick from underneath the goalposts by the defending side if the ball is:

- kicked or carried over the dead-ball line
- touched down by a defender
- kicked into touch on the full by a defender.

The game is restarted by a kick from the centre of the 20-metre line by the defending team if:

- the ball kicked over the dead-ball line or the touch-in-goal line by an attacker
- the attacking side infringes the laws in their opponent's in-goal area
- A defender catches the ball in the in-goal area before it bounces, after it has been kicked by the opposition in open play.

The ball is in play from the moment it is kicked. If, following a kick-off, the ball passes over the dead-ball line, whether it has touched a defending player or not, the game is restarted with a drop-out by a defending player from the centre of the goal line.

Where to take a scrum after a successful kick forward.

Where the scrum must take place if the ball goes out of play on the full.

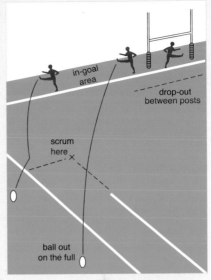

If a player punts the ball from behind the goal line and it bounces from the field of play into touch, a scrum is formed 20m in, level with the point where the ball crossed the touchline. The scrum feed is given to the non-kicking team. But if the ball goes directly into touch, the game is restarted with a drop-out from beneath the posts.

A player restarting the game with a drop kick.

SCORING RULES

The winning side in a rugby league match is the team that scores the most points. There are only two ways to score points: scoring tries and kicking goals.

SCORING TRIES

A try is scored by an attacking player placing the ball on the ground in his opponents' in-goal area providing the player is not:

- in touch himself
- in touch-in-goal
- over the dead-ball line.

The try is awarded at the spot where the player grounds the ball.

The referee may also award a try to a player if, in his opinion, the player would have scored but for unfair play by the defending team. In this case the try is awarded between the posts. It does not matter where the offence took place.

Sliding try

A try is awarded if a tackled player's momentum carries him into the opponents' in-goal, where he grounds the ball. This is commonly known as a 'sliding try' and will be awarded even if the ball has first touched the ground in the field of play. A try will not be awarded, though, if the player is touching the touchline or touch-in-goal line as he crosses the goal line, or is on or over the dead-ball line.

▼ This player keeps control of the ball as he dives into his opponent's in-goal area to score a try.

Remember
that the goal line
is part of and within
the in-goal area. This
means that a player
may score by placing
the ball on the
goal line.

OFFICIALS AND SPECTATORS

A try is awarded if an attacking player carrying the ball touches an official or spectator in his opponents' in-goal, the try being awarded at the point where the player touched the official or spectator.

SCORING GOALS

A goal is scored by kicking the ball from the field of play over the opponents' crossbar. A goal may be scored by:

- improving a try with a conversion kick
- a drop kick during play
- a penalty kick.

A goal cannot be scored from the following types of kicks:

- the kick-off kick
- a drop-out
- a punt
- a fly-kick which is a kick at a loose ball not held by any player.

A goal is allowed if the ball passes over the crossbar and is blown back by the wind. A goal is also scored if the ball hits the goal posts or crossbar providing it travels over the crossbar and between the posts.

A kick at goal
will not count if the
ball first bounces on
the ground before
travelling through
the posts.

This player is attempting a drop goal. If the ball touches a player on its route through the posts and over the crossbar, it is still allowed.

CONVERTING A TRY

A team scoring a try is awarded a kick at goal to attempt to 'improve' the try by a further two points. The kick at goal is taken from any point within the field of play opposite the spot where the try was awarded (see diagram below). The kick is a place kick which means that the ball is kicked from the ground.

Players of the defending side must stand behind their own goal line or outside the field of play. Players of the attacking side must remain behind the kicker until the kick has been taken.

After the kick at goal, the defending team restarts the game with a place kick from the centre of the halfway line whether the kick was successful or not.

EIGHT-POINT TRY

If a player fouls an opponent who is touching down for a try, the referee awards a penalty kick in addition to the conversion kick. The penalty kick is taken from in front of the posts after the attempt to convert the try has been made. This can potentially result in eight points (four for the try, two for the conversion and two for the penalty).

If you signal that you're going to kick for goal from a penalty, you must make a genuine attempt. You cannot deceive the opposition and start play with a tap kick instead.

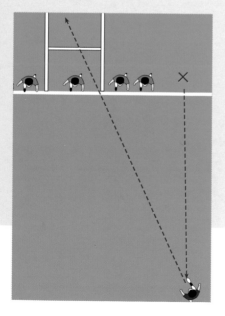

A conversion kick is taken in line with the position at which the try was scored.

GOAL FROM DROP KICK

A player may score a goal during play by dropping the ball and kicking it on the rebound so that it goes over the crossbar. This is known as a field goal and counts as one point.

GOAL FROM PENALTY KICK

Certain infringements (see pages 32–39) can result in the referee awarding a penalty kick. If the team awarded the kick choose to aim for goal, their kicker may place kick the ball from the ground or attempt a drop kick. A penalty kick at goal can be taken from any point on or behind the place where the offence occurred providing it is the same distance from the touchline.

Retreating opposition

The opposition team must retire 10m from the mark – the spot on the pitch where the penalty was awarded. If the penalty kicker moves the ball back a number of paces from the mark to improve his kicking angle, the opposition team can move forward so that they are 10m from the new mark.

This player has taken a penalty kick on goal. His team-mates had to stay behind the ball until it had been kicked.

PASSING RULES

The ball can be thrown or knocked from one player to another in any direction except forwards. It is not counted as an infringement if a player throws the ball sideways or backwards and it either falls to the ground, or is blown forwards by the wind. Play is allowed to continue.

FORWARD PASS

There are two types of forward pass – accidental and deliberate. If a player accidentally throws the ball in a forward direction to one of his own team, the referee awards a scrum at the place where the forward pass occurs. The team that did not make the forward pass get the feed into the scrum.

If the referee believes that the player was aware that his team-mate receiving the pass was forward of him, he should rule that the ball was deliberately passed forwards. He awards a penalty to the opposing team taken from where the forward pass occurred.

Making a pass count. This diagram shows a correct backward pass and an incorrect forward pass.

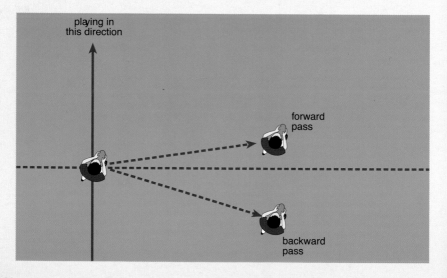

playing in
this direction

forward
pass

backward
pass

KNOCK-ON

A knock-on occurs when the ball, after touching the hand or arm of the player who was deliberately playing at the ball is dropped to the ground. For it to be a knock-on, the ball must travel in a forward direction (i.e. towards the opponents' goal line).

Play is allowed to proceed if:

- a player knocks the ball forwards and catches it again before it touches the ground

- a player knocks on and the opposing side gain an advantage such as possession of the ball.

If a player knocks on and the ball falls to the ground and he or any of his side gains an immediate advantage, for example his side regains possession, then play is stopped. The referee signals for a scrum to be formed.

 This ball has been kicked late, and is likely to be charged down by the no. 8 player.

A loose ball from a knock-on.

Charge down
A charge down is where a player manages to block an opponent's kick. Should a player charge down an opponent's kick and the ball rebound off his hand or arm, this isn't a knock-on and play is allowed to continue.

If your team makes a forward pass but an opponent gains possession before your team touches the ball, the game is allowed to continue.

TACKLING RULES

A player holding the ball may be tackled by an opponent. This means that he may be grasped round the body or legs in order to:

- bring him to the ground with the ball in his possession
- to stop his progress
- to prevent him from passing or kicking the ball.

HEAD AND HIGH TACKLES

It is an offence for a tackler to make any contact with the head of an opponent. The referee has to judge how serious the offence is. For example, a less serious offence such as where the tackler made a reflex action without any deliberate intent or when the tackled player ducked into the tackle might see a straightforward penalty awarded.

For more serious offences, however, the referee must dismiss the offending player from the field of play for 10 minutes (to the 'sin bin'). If the referee judges that the tackler made a deliberate and vicious attack to an opponent's head, he will dismiss the attacker for the remainder of the game.

 A tackle from behind.

POSSESSION IN THE TACKLE

If a player accidentally loses possession of the ball after he has been tackled, a scrum is formed on the spot. If he deliberately loses possession of the ball after being tackled a penalty shall be awarded against him.

Many tackles see the player with the ball go to ground. Some, though, will see him fairly held so that he cannot pass or kick the ball even though he has not been grounded. In this situation the referee may instruct him to play the ball (see pages 26-27).

If a number of players go down to ground together and the referee is undecided which player is in possession, he should order a scrum to be formed. A player should not deliberately allow himself to be tackled by falling to the ground or by dropping on to the ball and remaining on it when he could regain his feet and continue play.

It is illegal for you to 'steal' the ball from an opponent who is being tackled by more than one of your team.

TACKLE POINT

A tackle is considered to have taken place at the point not where a tackler first touches his opponent but where the tackled player's forward momentum ends. For example, a player running at full speed and tackled from behind may slide along the ground holding the ball for some distance. The tackle point is when he comes to a stop. So, if that distance travelled forward sees him crossing the opponent's goal line, a try may be scored.

Keeping possession of the ball while being tackled is a crucial skill. If the ball is lost before the tackled player is grounded, it can result in a scrum, with the feed going to the opposition.

HANDING OFF

A player may avoid a tackle being made on him by 'handing off' his opponent. This means he may push him off with the open palm of his hand. He must not strike or punch. A player who is tackled and held must play the ball.

PLAYING THE BALL

Bringing the ball back into play after a tackle is called playing or play-the-ball. The team in possession of the ball are allowed five play-the-balls in a row. If a team are tackled for the sixth time in a row and the ball has not been touched by an opponent, then possession of the ball is surrendered to the opposing team.

Play-the-ball process
When play is restarted with a play-the-ball, it is done in the following way.

1. The tackler must release his opponent without delay and the player in possession must play the ball as quickly as possible.

2. He regains his feet, faces his opponents' goal line, and places the ball in front of him, after which the ball must be played backward.

3. One opponent, not necessarily the tackler, may stand opposite the player playing the ball. He may stand as close as he likes. He must not, however, interfere with the movements of the player in possession.

> When playing the ball, make sure you have an acting half back in position. Make the half back aware as you roll the ball back.

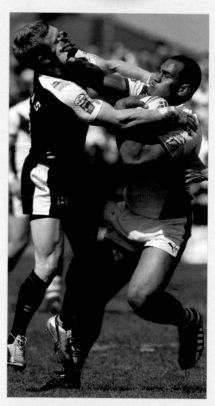

This player performs an excellent hand-off with the open palm of his hand to keep the tackler away.

Acting half backs

A player playing the ball more often than not heels the ball to a colleague standing behind him. This colleague is known as an acting half back. He may stand as close to the player playing the ball as he wishes provided he is directly behind.

The defending side is also allowed an acting half back. All other defending players are out of play if they have not retired 10m behind their own player who is taking part in the play-the-ball.

PROVIDING A MARKER

Judging whether you have retired the full 10m from a play-the-ball situation should be helped by the referee. He is advised to stand 10m from the play-the-ball situation on the defending team's side so that he provides a marker.

Playing the ball: the player in possession heels the ball to the acting half back.

SCRUM RULES

A scrum or scrummage is formed to restart the game in many situations. Up to six players from each team may be part of each side's scrum.

FORMING A SCRUM

The scrum is formed in most cases where the infringement occurred, but must never be less than 20m in from the touchline or closer than 20m from the goal line. When a scrum offence occurs, the penalty is awarded where the scrum should have formed in the first place.

THE PACK

A team's players in a scrum are known as a pack. A normal pack consists of:

- three forwards in the front row of a scrum
- two in the second row
- one loose forward who is positioned between the second row forwards with his shoulders pushing against their buttocks.

The front row forwards of each team bind together with their arms. They also interlock arms and heads with the opposing front row forwards in order to form a clear tunnel between the rows. The tunnel formed is at right angles to the touchline.

Loose head

The one front row forward who packs nearest to the referee is known as the loose head. The non-offending side must always have the loose head. The one exception is when a scrum is formed because of a rules infringement by both sides. In this case, the attacking side are given the loose head.

THE SCRUM HALF

The scrum half of the non-offending side feeds the scrum by rolling the ball along the ground into the centre of the tunnel from the side on which the referee is standing. He must then immediately retire behind his own pack of forwards.

THE HOOKER

When the ball hits the ground in the tunnel the two hookers may 'strike' for the ball with either foot. Their aim is to heel the ball back to their scrum half. All other forwards must keep both feet on the ground. The hooker should pack with both arms over the shoulders of the two supporting front row forwards. The ball must emerge from the scrum between and behind the second row of forwards to be in play.

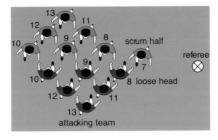

attacking team

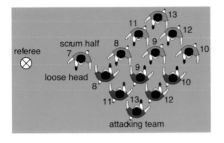

attacking team

BEHIND THE SCRUM

The other players in a team not involved in a scrum must retire 5m or more behind the last row of forwards of their team in the scrum. They must keep their distance until the ball has emerged correctly from the scrum. If they do not, a differential penalty (see page 33) may be awarded where the scrum was formed.

This diagram shows the correct formation for all scrums, with the loose head of the attacking team on the same side as the referee.

The paths that the ball can take as it leaves the scrum, having been fed in by the scrum half (no. 7).

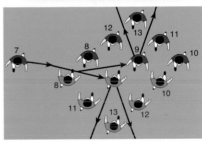

Until the ball comes out from the back of the scrum, nobody can touch it. Once it emerges, either the scrum half or the loose forward can pick it up and start a new attack.

KICKING RULES

There are three types of kick employed in the game – the punt, the drop kick and the place kick.

THE PUNT

A player is said to punt the ball when he drops it from his hands and kicks it before it touches the ground. A punt may be made in any direction and is useful for finding touch or gaining ground. The key rule that applies to the punt kick is that a goal cannot be scored from it.

To make a good punt, the ball is kicked with the instep of the boot (where the laces are). An expert kicker may attempt a torpedo punt. This is an advanced variation where the kicker imparts a spiralling movement to the ball which helps it rifle through the air with greater distance and accuracy.

THE DROP KICK

A player drop kicks the ball when he drops it from his hands to the ground and kicks it immediately it rebounds on the half-volley. A drop kick is used to:

- restart the game after dead ball from an unsuccessful penalty kick at goal and after certain other dead-ball situations
- to score a goal during play. A drop goal counts one point.

THE PLACE KICK

A place kick is made by a player placing the ball on the ground and then running forwards and kicking it. It is used to:

- start the game and restart it after half-time or points have been scored
- kick at goal after a try has been scored
- kick at goal after the award of a penalty kick.

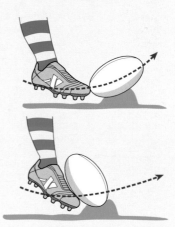

There are various ways of place kicking the ball. Here are the two most popular techniques – kicking with the toe of the boot (above) and kicking with the instep (below).

A useful
aid to accuracy
when place kicking
is to aim a seam of
the ball at the
target.

RAISING THE BALL

The laws of the game
permit the kicker to raise
the ball from the ground
using a form of tee.
Traditionally, this was
soil and grass dug by the
kicker's boot. Today, many
kickers prefer to use a
mound of sand or a plastic
tee on which to sit the ball.

▼ If a kick is allowed to bounce
and goes loose, it can be a
scramble for the defending team to
secure the ball.

THE PENALTY KICK

The referee awards a penalty kick to the non-offending team when the following groups of infringements occur:

- deliberate disobedience of the laws

- foul play (see page 34)

- obstruction (see page 35)

- offside play (see pages 36–39)

- technical offences at the scrum.

The penalty kick may be a drop kick, a place kick or a punt, and is taken at any point on or behind the spot where the infringement occurred and the same distance from the touchline.

This player uses a plastic kicking tee to place the ball to take a penalty kick. He carefully aligns the ball with his target and will focus on the part of the ball he will kick throughout the approach to the kick.

Rules

When the penalty kick is taken, the following rules must be observed:

- all players of the kicker's side must be behind the ball when it is kicked

- players of the offending side must retire 10m, towards their own goal line, from the mark

- players of the offending side must not charge the kick, or raise their hands above their heads.

If a player signals that he intends to kick at goal from a penalty, he must make a genuine attempt and not signal to deceive the opposition.

Infringing at penalty kicks

For an infringement by the kicker's team the referee awards a scrum at the point where the kick was awarded.

For an infringement by the offending team the kick is either retaken or another penalty is awarded where the offence took place. The referee decides which of the above awards give the non-offending side the most advantage.

Aim of the kick

The object of a penalty kick may be to:

- score a goal from a drop kick or place kick

- restart play without delay by kicking the ball in any direction from the mark and keeping the ball in the field of play

- gain ground by kicking for touch.

After a successful kick for touch, the kicker's side is allowed to place the ball on the ground 10m in from the point of entry into touch. They then restart play with another kick. A goal cannot be scored so usually the player taking it tap kicks and then keeps possession for his side.

This player takes a tap penalty, kicking the ball to himself before passing to a team-mate to begin an attack.

Differential penalty

For technical offences at the scrum (for example, foot up, illegal binding, improper feeding or offside by any player), the differential penalty operates. The non-offending side may either kick for touch or take a tap kick. They may not, however, kick at goal.

FOULS AND OBSTRUCTION

There are three main forms of foul play. A penalty is awarded against a player committing foul play and against some obstruction offences.

TRIPPING

A player is not allowed to trip an opponent with his foot. The referee may order the offender from the field of play.

STRIKING

A player is not allowed to strike, or attempt to strike, an opponent with his fist or any part of his arm. The referee may order the offender from the field of play.

KICKING

A player is not allowed to:

- kick at an opponent
- kick recklessly at the ball when an opponent is picking it up
- kick recklessly at the ball when it might cause injury to an opponent.

In all the above cases, the referee may order the offender from the field of play.

◄ The player on the left may be penalised for pushing his opponent away from the ball before he had gathered it.

► Glenn Morrison of Bradford Bulls being tackled by two players from French club Catalans Dragons, 2007.

OBSTRUCTION

A player is obstructing an opponent if he deliberately:

- impedes his progress when running towards the ball
- tackles him after he has kicked the ball, thus preventing him from following up the kick
- tackles or impedes any player who is not in possession of the ball.

For these offences a penalty is awarded.

> **When you and an opposition player are running side by side towards a ball, you are allowed to use a shoulder charge but not your hands or arms.**

Tackling after a kick

It is often difficult for a player to halt a tackle made just as the opponent is about to kick, and it is left to the referee's discretion whether the tackle was made deliberately after the kick or not. If a penalty is given, it is awarded where the ball bounces (if kicked forwards), or 10m from the touchline opposite to where it leaves the field of play if it is kicked out on the full.

Obstruction out of play

If obstruction offences warranting penalties occur in touch then the offenders can still be penalised. The mark is made 10m infield from the touchline level with where the offence occurred.

Penalty kicks are taken from various other places.

- A penalty kick resulting from an offence at the kick-off is taken from the centre of the halfway line.
- Any penalty kick arising from the restarting of play from the 20-metre line is taken from the centre of that line.
- Penalty kicks resulting from an offence at the goal line drop-out are taken from the centre of the line 10m from the goal line.
- If a defending side makes a penalty offence in its own in-goal, the mark is made in the field of play 10m from the goal line and opposite where the offence was committed.

OFFSIDE

A player is in an offside position anywhere between his goal line and the opponents' dead-ball line when he is in front of a team-mate who has the ball, or who last touched the ball. Any player who is not nearer to his own goal line than the tackled player shall be offside. Such a player is penalised if he gains or attempts to gain an unfair advantage.

NON-INTERFERENCE

An offside player must not take any part in the game or attempt in any way to influence the course of the game. He must not encroach within 10m of an opponent who is waiting for the ball. He must also retire 10m immediately from any opponent who first secures possession.

PENALTY AWARD

The referee may award a penalty kick to the opposing team when a player is in an offside position and performs one of the three following actions:

- plays or attempts to play the ball
- tackles or attempts to play the ball
- tackles or attempts to tackle an opponent.

The penalty kick is awarded where the infringement occurred.

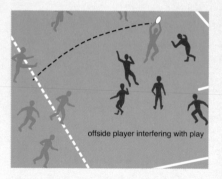

offside player interfering with play

In this diagram, there are four players in blue who are offside as their team-mate kicks the ball ahead. The player who catches the ball is offside and interfering with play, and will be penalised by the referee.

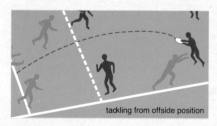

tackling from offside position

This diagram shows a player in blue in an offside position tackling an opponent with the ball.

> **Never argue with a referee. The referee's decision and word are final.**

OFFSIDE AT KICK-OFFS AND DROP-OUTS

When offside play occurs at a kick-off or a drop-out, a penalty kick is awarded at the centre of the appropriate line or, in the case of a drop-out from between the posts, the penalty is awarded 10m from the goal line and mid-way between the posts.

In this situation, two players, **A** and **B**, are ahead of their team-mate who is in possession of the ball. The two players are offside.

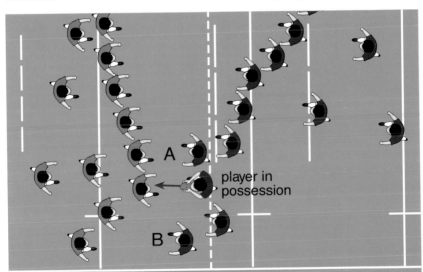

A

player in possession

B

REFEREE'S SIGNALS

When the game is stopped, it is the duty of the referee to signal his decision and, where necessary, the nature of the infringement.

These signals are of great benefit both to players and spectators who can quickly pick up and understand the referee's decision. It is worth taking time to learn all the referee's signals.

 Penalty kick awarded.

 Obstruction.

PLACED ONSIDE

A player in an offside position can be placed onside in some situations. For this to occur, he must not be within 10m of an opponent who has possession of the ball and one of the following movements has occurred:

- an opponent in possession of the ball has run 10m
- the ball has been kicked or passed by an opponent
- a player of his own side in possession of the ball has run in front of him
- a team-mate in possession of the ball kicks the ball when behind him and then runs in front of him. If the kicker follows up by running into touch, he must return to the field of play before he can put other players onside.

 The prop has raised his foot to strike for the ball in a scrum.

 Dissent (arguing or verbally abusing the referee).

 The scrum half has fed his own feet.

 Forward pass.

If you think you see opponents offside, do not assume the referee will stop the game. He may allow play to proceed if he thinks your side, the non-offending side, have an advantage.

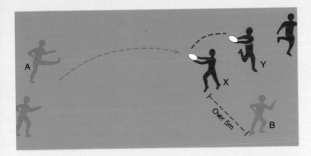

Player **B** is offside when his team-mate kicks the ball and it is caught by the opponent, player **X**. When **X** passes the ball to **Y**, player **B** is now onside.

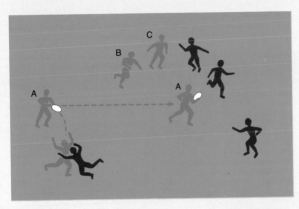

When player **A** receives the ball, his team-mates, **B** and **C** are both offside. By running forwards and ahead of them, if he passes to either **B** or **C**, they will be onside.

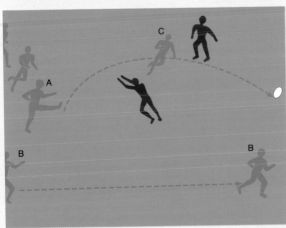

Player **A** kicks the ball forward and player **B** sprints ahead. Only the kicker (player **A**) can put the offside player (player **C**) onside.

BASIC SKILLS: RUNNING AND PASSING

Rugby league is essentially a running game in which retaining possession of the ball is crucial. A player running with the ball should hold it firmly in both hands ready to make a swift pass. If however, a player is attempting to beat an opponent's tackle, the ball will usually be carried close to the centre of the body, using one hand and the forearm.

A fast, accurate pass is a key rugby league skill. Learning and practising the right technique is an important part of any player's training.

PASSING THE BALL

Accurate passing of the ball is the key to breaking the opposition's defence and setting up scoring positions.

The ball is held with fingers spread underneath the ball and thumbs on the upper part of the ball, holding it in position. Arms are relaxed, with elbows slightly bent and close to the side, so that the ball can be swung and passed in either direction, left or right.

Apart from a good grip, the following are technique tips to ensure an accurate pass:

- the upper part of the body should twist at the hips

- the shoulders come round square to the receiver

- the arms swing the ball back, and then move across the body

- aim to release the ball towards the target area with a flat trajectory

- the ball's path is directed by the fingers and wrists
- the arms follow-through fully extended in the direction of the intended receiver.

RECEIVING THE BALL

All players must be able to receive a pass as well as execute one. Concentration is important as is the ability to react to a pass that is not aimed in the perfect place.

To receive a pass, the player's upper body turns to face the passer with the eyes firmly fixed on the ball as it leaves the passer's hands. The arms and the fingers are extended towards the ball in its flight. Whenever possible, both hands should be used to receive the ball and secure possession.

PASSING FROM THE GROUND

This sort of pass is used at many play-the-ball and scrum situations. The passer must judge the distance and position of the receiver and judge the right amount of force with which to make the pass. The ball is directed by the fingers and wrists with a clear follow-through by the arms towards the receiver.

RUNNING ATTITUDE

At all times, the first thoughts of a player with the ball in space should be to run straight and with great determination. An ability to 'read the game' – knowing where opponents and one's own supporting players are – is extremely important.

A well-judged and executed pass means that the receiver can collect the ball without reducing their speed. This helps keep an attack going and can lead to tries.

Remember, as a passer, the target area is in front of the intended receiver at around chest height. Do not lob the ball.

BASIC SKILLS: EVASION

Rugby league is an exciting spectator sport. Much of its appeal comes from the individual skills used by players to beat the intended tackles of their opponents. Such moves can find and generate space for exciting running and free-flowing passing.

METHODS OF EVASION

The most widely used methods of evasion are:

- the sidestep
- the swerve
- the hand-off
- the bump-off
- the hit and spin
- changes of pace
- the dummy.

THE SIDESTEP

The sidestep involves a sudden change of direction to beat an opponent who is already committed to making a tackle. The player's head should remain still throughout the movement. He should not shorten his stride as he approaches the defender.

To sidestep to the left, the toes of the right foot are driven hard into the ground. The runner thrusts himself sideways. He transfers his weight to the left foot which is driven hard into the ground on contact. This enables the runner to continue on a straight running line but in a new direction, leaving the defender in his wake.

For the sidestep to the right, the opposite actions apply. Good players should be able to sidestep in both directions.

A defender is left lunging in the wrong direction as a result of a well-timed sidestep. To be most effective, the sidestep should be executed at maximum speed.

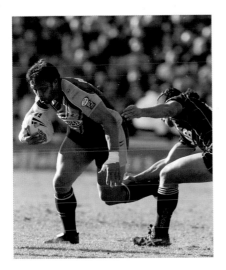

This player keeps his balance at a good pace to swerve round a defender.

THE SWERVE

The swerve involves the runner changing direction to take him round the would-be tackler. The movement is left late but it is not as extreme as the sidestep. Good footwork and timing are vital.

To swerve to the right, the runner balances on the outside of his right foot and the inside of his left. He runs in a curve away from his would-be tackler with his hips also swaying to the right and away from his opponent.

For a swerve to the left, the player balances on the outside of his left foot and the inside of his right, with his route and hips swaying away to the right side of his opponent.

THE HAND-OFF

A hand-off requires accurate timing to enable the attacker to either push the tackler away and down, or to use the defender's own momentum to propel the attacker away. To execute an effective hand-off, the player with the ball performs the following actions:

- he transfers the ball to one hand

- he makes a strong thrust with his other arm

- using an open palm facing outwards, he pushes or fends off with a forceful stabbing motion

- he usually makes contact with the chest, head or shoulder

- he straightens his arm immediately on contact.

Work hard in training to learn to combine a hand-off with a sidestep or swerve. Used together, this pair of actions can be very effective in evading opponents.

THE BUMP-OFF

The bump-off is a method of breaking a tackle. A player uses a hard part of the body, particularly the shoulder or the hip, to knock or bump off the would-be tackler.

The player with the ball must run with great determination. At the moment of contact, the legs must be driven hard into the ground in order to generate the necessary force and momentum to carry the runner through the intended tackle. Once the bump-off has occurred, the player should try to sprint away.

HIT AND SPIN

Similar to the bump-off, the hit and spin sees the ball-carrier dip his shoulder at the point of contact – known as the collision point. He uses this movement to turn and spin off and away from the defender. From this point he can continue to make ground himself or pass the ball to a supporting team-mate.

The runner should take short steps as the collision point approaches. The player's legs should pump vigorously throughout the action. This helps generate the power to drive round and away from the defender.

CHANGE OF PACE

The ball-carrier always holds a potential advantage over his opponents. Only he knows what he intends to do next in order to beat the would-be tackler. Deceiving an opponent can create uncertainty in his mind. He may be caught between two actions and do neither of them well.

Change of pace involves a sudden acceleration which causes the defender to mistime his tackle. As he approaches the would-be tackler, the player slows down a little causing the defender to alter his positioning and adjust his timing for the tackle. The player then moves suddenly into top gear, lengthening his stride and accelerating quickly away.

Practice dummies, changes of pace and other evasive moves in training with team-mates. The more confident you are with such moves the more likely you are to succeed.

Eyes fixed on a gap in the defence, this player accelerates off his left foot in an attempt to break the gain line.

THE DUMMY

To execute a dummy pass, the ball-carrier acts as if he is really about to make a pass, but instead holds onto the ball and continues running. For this move to work, the dummy must be completely convincing with the arms following through as if making the pass, so that the defender truly believes the pass will occur. A deceived defender is likely to glance and move towards the likely receiver giving you a vital split-second to sprint clear.

CHEST BUMP-OFF

The chest may also be used to bump off a defender. In this technique, the ball-carrier folds his arms over the ball, elbows downwards, with the brunt of the impact being taken on his forearms.

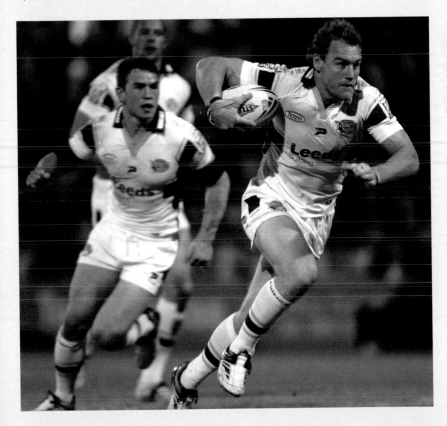

BASIC SKILLS: PLAY-THE-BALL

The play-the-ball is a unique and totally distinctive feature of rugby league football. The move is used to restart play immediately following a completed tackle.

STANDING UP

In order to play the ball, the tackled player must first regain his feet as quickly as possible. How fast he can do this depends on his landing position. For example, being on your elbows and knees is a position you can quickly lever yourself up from. In contrast, lying on your back is a position which will take a second or two longer to get up from.

PLAYING-THE-BALL

Facing the opposition goal line, the player lifts the ball clear of the ground. Bending his body well over the ball, he places it lengthways on the ground in front of and alongside his leading foot. At the same time, the sole of his other foot is placed on top of the ball.

Using the sole of his boot, the ball is rolled back under complete control to a team-mate behind him, known as the acting half back. This player must collect the ball quickly and smoothly and has the option of either passing directly from the ground to a team-mate – dubbed the first receiver – or to run with the ball himself.

A SIMPLE SKILL

Playing-the-ball is a simple, straightforward move yet it is bungled on a surprisingly large number of occasions. Some 300 or more play-the-balls take place in every game. For the team in possession to sustain continuous attacks it is vital that each play-the-ball in a 'set of six' is quickly and smoothly executed. Every player should work hard to master the skill and in a match situation, concentrate as they perform this skill.

PLAYING IT YOURSELF

The ball must be played backwards into the hands of the acting half back. If the defence is caught napping by a particularly quick play-the-ball, and does not provide a marker, the player playing the ball may play it to himself by tapping it forwards into his own hands and thus continuing the attack.

The ball is rolled carefully backwards to his acting half back using the player's stronger, more reliable foot.

The acting half back, having collected the ball smoothly, passes quickly to the first receiver.

This player has stood up quickly and has placed the ball in the correct position ready to play-the-ball.

BASIC SKILLS: TACKLING

Although rugby league is essentially a running and handling game, strong, well-organised and totally committed defence is the foundation of a winning team.

TACKLING SKILLS

Effective tackling requires accurate timing, good technique, determination and, as smaller players must often tackle larger players moving at speed, bravery. Players may make a tackle or be tackled as frequently as between twenty and forty times during a full game. Mastering tackle techniques will enable players of all sizes to tackle successfully and often without injury.

BASIC TACKLES

There are four basic tackles which all players must strive to master. These are:

- tackles from the side
- tackles from the rear
- front tackles
- smother tackles.

The side, rear and front tackles all aim to knock the ball-carrier to the ground. The smother tackle is different. The smother tackle's aim is to pinion the ball-carrier's arms so that he cannot pass to a supporting team-mate.

SIDE AND REAR TACKLES

Certain important elements are common requirements for tackles made from the side or from the rear. These are as follows:

- the target area is your opponent's thigh
- approach the tackle by correctly positioning the oncoming ball-carrier
- keep your hands up and keep your head up
- contact the ball-carrier by stepping into them
- hit the target area with your shoulder, gripping and circling the ball-carrier's thighs at the same time
- upon completion of the tackle, the tackler should endeavour to finish on top of the ball-carrier and regain his feet first, thus ready for the next phase of play.

An excellent side-on tackle stops the opponent with the ball in his tracks and sends him to ground quickly. See how the tackler's head is behind his opponent.

Head Position

The position of the tackler's head is extremely important in helping to guarantee a successful rear or side tackle is made as well as ensuring that the tackler himself is not hurt whilst tackling.

For the orthodox tackle from the side, the head must always be placed behind the opponent.

For the tackle from the rear, the head should be placed at the side of the opponent, and as the hands link to secure a firm hold they should be slid down the ball-carrier's legs.

Work with your coach on the tackling technique using crash mats to cushion the fall. This helps build confidence.

FRONT-ON TACKLES

Because many of the physical confrontations in rugby league are head-to-head, it is absolutely essential that all players learn to tackle from a front-on position.

Tackling an opponent from the front who is moving at pace can be daunting for some younger and less experienced players. It is important to remember, that making a safe and successful front-on tackle is not all about great size and bulk, it is far more about the tackler's technique, determination, commitment and timing.

TYPES OF TACKLE

There are two types of head-on tackle:

- a more passive version, in which the tackler uses his opponent's own weight and momentum against him
- a more aggressive version, known as the drive tackle, in which the ball-carrier is lifted and forced backwards in a powerful drive by the tackler.

THE DRIVE TACKLE

In executing the drive tackle, you should use exactly the same approach, contact and finish principles that you made to tackles from the rear and side, with the only exceptions being as follows:

- the target area should be your opponent's waist
- your head should be to the side of the ball-carrier
- your arms should encircle the ball-carrier's body under their buttocks and below their centre of gravity
- drive powerfully with your legs; at the same time pull and lift your opponent, using your arms and shoulders to drive them backwards onto the ground.

This player has performed an excellent front-on tackle. See how his arm is pinning the ball to the attacking player's chest.

THE SMOTHER TACKLE

When a tackler is isolated and cannot rely on a team-mate to smother the opponent to prevent him releasing the ball, a smother tackle can be used. A determined tackle with a firm clamping of the ball-carrier's arms, will often succeed in preventing the ball being transferred to another opponent in support.

For the smother tackle to be effective, the same general principles used in the approach, contact and finish phases of the other tackles again apply, but you should also keep in mind the following:

• the target area is the ball

• arms must be wrapped around the upper part of the ball-carrier's body to trap the ball against their body

• the tackle is completed by wrestling your opponent to the floor.

The most effective smother tackle is likely to be made when the tackler approaches his opponent from the outside.

SMOTHERING THE BALL

It is most important that an opponent, even when tackled, should not be allowed to offload the ball to a supporting team-mate. Therefore, the second player into the tackle must have the ability to smother the ball by circling and pinning the opponent's arms so that the ball is trapped against the body and cannot be passed.

 A smother tackle, wrapping up the ball so that it cannot be quietly recycled.

BASIC SKILLS: KICKING

Though rugby league is essentially a game based on running, passing and tackling, kicking, especially as a tactical ploy and to score points is also important.

TYPES OF KICK

Most teams have specialist kickers, but all players should master the basic kicking skills applied to five types of kick:

- the punt
- the grubber
- the kick-over or chip
- the drop kick
- the place kick.

This player has hit a punt with his shoulders square to the target and his head down watching the ball.

THE PUNT

The punt is a kick from hand used to gain ground from either a penalty kick or in open play. A very high version of the kick is used in attack to send the ball behind the opposition's defence line and deep into the opponent's half for team-mates to chase.

1. The ball is held as if making a pass.

2. The hands guide the ball down to the point where contact is made with the foot.

3. The ankle should be flexed on contact, straightening the toes.

4. The foot drives through the ball after contact, with a full follow-through of the kicking leg towards the target.

THE GRUBBER KICK

The aim of this short kick is to slot the ball between opposition players and move it into space behind the opponent's defensive line. Ideally, the ball rolls end-over-end for a team-mate to run through and collect.

The foot makes contact with the top of the ball just before it hits the ground. The player's head is over the ball and the foot stabs at the ball with no follow through to send it into the ground.

THE KICK-OVER OR CHIP KICK

This kick, like the grubber, is used to break a well-organised defence but by kicking the ball over the heads of defenders. The basic technique is similar to the punt except that the kicking foot is slightly flexed and does not follow through. The ball should travel only a short distance, so hitting the ball with the correct amount of force (known as a kick's weight) is vital.

THE DROP KICK

The drop kick is used for restarts or for scoring one point by kicking the ball over the bar from broken play. The key difference to the punt is that the foot makes contact with the ball just as it touches the ground.

The ball is held and guided to the ground at an angle of around 45 degrees. It should land beside the toes of the non-kicking foot. With the eyes watching the ball right through the kick, the ball is struck with the lower part of the instep.

This player executes a chip kick to put the ball into space behind his opponents. The chip kick is a skill that top players learn to execute when moving at speed.

To hit a restart drop kick, delay your foot's contact with the ball a fraction to add greater distance to the kick.

This player makes a drop kick. His arms are spread to help keep his balance and his body leant back slightly.

THE PLACE KICK

The place kick is used to start and restart a game, or to kick for goal. There are two main methods used to take a place kick. The traditional toe-end kick and the round-the-corner method. Both have strengths and weaknesses.

The toe-end method

The kicker, ball and target are all in a straight line so good technique is likely to ensure accuracy. On the negative side, the point of impact (the toe of the foot) is small meaning that there is little margin for error.

1. Standing with kicking foot directly behind the ball and non-kicking foot beside it, the kicker checks that he, the ball and the target are all in line.

2. With head bent, and eyes on the spot on the ball where he intends making contact, the kicker takes his preferred number of steps backwards from the ball.

3. Concentrating hard, the kicker moves slowly forwards staying balanced.

4. With the body well over the ball and head bent, the toe makes contact with the foot and kicking leg following through powerfully directly towards the target.

This player takes a place kick using the round-the-corner method. His shoulders are square to the target and his non-kicking foot beside the ball.

When catching a high ball, concentrate solely on the flight of the ball. Judge the flight and move quickly into position to receive the ball.

The round-the-corner method

The kicker approaches the ball using a curved run-up with the final two strides being straight on to the ball. He strikes it with the instep, as if kicking a soccer ball.

This method allows the kicker to obtain greater distance.

Apart from the run-up, the round-the-corner method is similar to the toe-end except:

- the ball should be struck with the instep or inside of the foot

- the non-kicking foot is placed slightly further away from the ball, allowing the hip and thigh to swing through.

CATCHING A HIGH BALL

Kicking has become an important tactic in rugby league, and all players must be able to deal with the kind of attacking kick known as a bomb or up-and-under in which the ball is propelled high into the air.

1. Get into position with arms outwards and upwards, fingers spread.

2. Guide the ball safely into a cradle formed by the hands, forearms and chest.

3. As the ball is secured, get elbows in, round the shoulders and bend the knees.

4. Turn your side into the opponents who will have followed the high kick to keep the ball secure.

For a place kick, the ball should sit on the tee so that a central point around 25mm from the bottom of the ball can be seen. This is where the ball will be kicked.

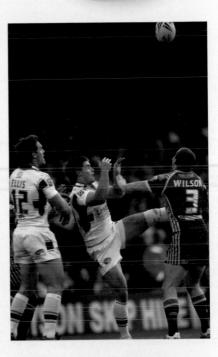

Players aiming to catch a high ball must watch it all the way into their hands. Taking your eye off the ball often results in dropping it.

BASIC SKILLS: SCRUMMAGING

Possession of the ball is vital in rugby league and good scrummaging technique can secure the ball for your side. A scrum usually consists of a set of six forwards per side bending together in a 3-2-1, triangular-shaped formation.

FORMING A SCRUM

At a scrummage, the front row forwards bind tightly together, side-by-side, leaving no gaps between them.

They interlock their arms and heads with their opponents to form a clear tunnel.

The two second row forwards bind tightly together and then enter the scrum by packing down behind the front row, placing their heads in the gaps between the hooker and the prop forwards. The loose forward packs down behind the second row forwards, inserting his head between them, using his arms to bind the two second row forwards securely together.

BODY POSITION

When the scrum is formed the bodies of all the forwards involved should be as far as possible horizontal to the ground, thus enabling them to push with the maximum forward momentum. Once the scrum has been correctly formed, both packs are permitted to push.

STRIKING THE BALL

The scrum half awarded the ball feeds it into the tunnel formed by the scrum. At this point, both hookers may strike for the ball. The hooker of the side whose scrum half puts the ball in has two advantages:

- through agreed signals or speech, he will know the timing of the feed into the scrum

- his feet are closer to the ball because his prop nearest to the scrum half is positioned as a 'loose head' with his head outside his opposite number.

EFFECTIVE SCRUMMAGING

The following principles help with good scrummaging.

1. The hooker tries to arrive first at the spot where the scrum will take place (the mark).

2. The other scrum forwards should follow quickly and aim to bind up before their opponents have done so.

3. Once the ball has been fed into the scrum, the surest way of gaining possession is by means of a strong forward push by all forwards at the same time, save the hooker. He must time a quick, decisive strike for the ball.

4. The scrum half moves quickly to a position behind the scrum and must stay alert. The ball is in play once it has been raked back through the scrummage to emerge between and behind the feet of the second row forwards.

▼ The front row of a scrum features two prop forwards with their hooker supported between them. The hooker's job is to secure possession of the ball by heeling it backwards through the scrum.

SCRUMMAGING SUCCESS

In order to perfect the timing of the push and a decisive strike of the ball, regular practice involving the forwards and scrum half is essential.

- The scrum half and forwards must understand when the ball is going to be fed into the scrum.

- The forwards, particularly the front row, must develop their all-round strength, paying special attention to their upper body, shoulders and neck.

MODIFIED GAMES

The Rugby League Coach Education Programme has created the Modified Games Programme. These are scaled-down versions of the full game which are safe, enjoyable and relatively simple. These games help youngsters learn and understand the basic rules, skills and tactics. The two versions are Mini League for seven to nine year olds and Mod League for 10- and 11-year-olds.

MINI LEAGUE RULES

Number of players
The maximum number of players per team is nine. There is no limit to the amount of substitutions, but each player must play at least half a whole game.

Duration
All games should be played in two halves of seven-and-a-half minutes maximum with a two-minute interval. No player should be allowed to play for more than a total of 40 minutes in any one day.

Ball and playing area
The game is played with a Mini League ball or size three standard rugby league ball. The playing area should be a maximum of 60 x 40m and a minimum of 50 x 30m. Mini League can be played on any grassed area.

One of the joys of playing rugby league is that all players have a chance to run with the ball.

Tackles

The normal six-tackle rule applies. However, after each tackle all players must retire 5m prior to the play-the-ball restart. The tackled player should restart the game by way of a play-the-ball. The ball must be played backwards in the correct manner where the tackle occurred.

The defending side cannot move until the ball is passed by the acting half back or the acting half back runs with the ball. The minimum distance the ball is played from the try line is 5m. If the acting half back is tackled in possession of the ball, it will result in a hand over of possession to the opposition.

It is important players enjoy playing rugby league; running with the ball is a big part of being involved in the game.

Scoring

A try is scored in the normal way by placing or touching the ball down on or over the opponents' try line.

Kicking

Kicking the ball is not allowed except after a try has been awarded when the scoring team will take a place kick conversion in front of the goalposts. No player is allowed to make more than one attempt at goal until every other player has had an attempt.

Scrums

All scrums are passive, with any team attempting to push or rotate the scrum being penalised. Referees should instruct the teams at the scrum to crouch, engage and hold.

MOD LEAGUE RULES

Number of players
The number of players per team is eleven (five forwards and six backs), with as many substitutes as are needed. Each player must play at least half a whole game.

Duration
The game is played in two halves. The maximum length of each half is 20 minutes with a five-minute interval.

Concentration is essential during a game of rugby league. This potential star of the future keeps his eyes fixed firmly on the ball.

Ball and playing area
The game is played with a Mod League ball or size four standard rugby league ball. The maximum pitch dimensions are 80m long by 50m wide. Goalposts should be padded and situated outside the field of play.

Number of tackles
The normal six-tackle rule applies and the tackled player restarts the game with a play-the-ball. The ball must be played backwards in the correct manner and where the tackle occurred.

All defending players must retire 10m at the play-the-ball, except for a single marker who must be square to the player playing the ball. He or she cannot interfere at any stage of the play-the-ball and cannot move until the acting half back runs with the ball.

If the acting half back is tackled in possession of the ball, it will result in a hand over of possession to the opposition.

Scoring
A try is scored in the normal way, with a player placing or touching the ball down on or over their opponents' try line.

Kicking
Kicking is allowed after a try has been scored. The kick should be taken no more than 10m from each side of the posts. No player is allowed a second kick at goal until every other player in the team has had an attempt.

The scrum

A passive scrum shall be formed by no less than five players from each team. It should be no nearer than 10m from all touchlines or the try line.

The team not responsible for making the ball go out of play will have the advantage of head and feed.

The scrum half must feed the ball in the correct way into the tunnel of the scrum. Both scrum halves must retire behind their forwards' rear feet. The ball should leave the scrum through a 'tunnel' of the second row forward's legs in accordance with the rules of the game.

SCRUM WHEN BALL IN TOUCH

If the ball goes into touch, the scrum has to form 10m within the field of play. It must form opposite the point where the ball last made contact with either the field of play or a player. This rule does not apply within 10m of the goal line.

A player punts the ball in a Mod League game. Grubber, chip and punt kicks are allowed in open play but secondary kicking (e.g. fly kicking and dribbling) is not.

USEFUL ADDRESSES

RFL
Red Hall
Red Hall Lane
Leeds LS17 8NB
tel: 0844 477 7113
website: www.therfl.co.uk

British Amateur Rugby League Association
West Yorkshire House
4 New North Parade
Huddersfield HD1 5JP
tel: 01484 544131
website: www.barla.org.uk

Rugby League International Federation
PO Box 533
Wakehurst Parkway
Narrabeen
NSW 2101
Australia
tel: 0061 2 9971 0877
website: www.rlif.org/

Australian Rugby League
GPO Box 4415
Sydney
NSW 2001
Australia
tel: 0061 2 9232 7566
website:
www.australianrugbyleague.com.au

Canadian Rugby Football League
PO Box 16086, Station 'F'
Ottawa, Ontario
Canada K2C 3S9
tel: 0016 1 3692 0572
email: dave_silcock_crfl@canada.com

Fédération Française de Rugby à XIII
30 Rue de l'Echiquier
75010 Paris
France
tel: 0033 1 4800 9256
website: www.ffr13.com

Japan Rugby League
8-10-15-701 Ginza Chuo-ku
Tokyo
Japan
tel: 0081 422 395 881
website: www.geocities.jp/
japaneserugbyleague/e/info.html

New Zealand Rugby League
Rugby League House
7 Beasley Avenue
Penrose
Auckland
New Zealand
tel: 0064 9 525 5592
website: www.nzrl.co.nz

Russian Rugby League Federation
24 (Sector B5)
Luzhnetskaya Naberezhnaya
Moscow
Russia
tel: 007 095 772 7852
website: www.rrl.ru/

South African Rugby League
Postnet Suite 453
Private Bag X2
Dunswart
Gauteng
South Africa 1613
tel: 0027 011 899 2055
website: www.sarugbyleague.co.za

INDEX